Disclaimer

The information provided herein is stated to be truthful and consistent, in that any liability, in terms of inattention or otherwise, by any usage or abuse of any policies, processes, or directions contained within is the solitary and utter responsibility of the recipient reader.

The information herein is offered for informational purposes solely, and is universal as so. The presentation of the information is without contract or any type of guarantee assurance.

Under no circumstances will any legal responsibility or blame be held against the author or publisher for any reparation, damages, or monetary loss due to the information herein, either directly or indirectly.

Before Getting Started

First and foremost thank you for purchasing my cookbook. Many well-established kitchen gurus have helped with crafting these unique recipes and without their contributions this would not be possible. I sincerely hope you enjoy it.

Also, if you would be kind enough to leave a positive review on Amazon it would be greatly appreciated. You have no idea how much it helps us independent authors!

Your friend,
Carla

P.S. — Please be sure to download your **FREE DIGITAL COPY OF THE BOOK!**

Table of Contents

Mù Xū Pork Styled Burger

Vegetarian Chipotle Burger

Western Roasted Red Burger

Burgers & Mexican Yam Slaw

Apple Bacon Burger

Smoky Southern–Style Burger

George–on–Diet Burger

Apocalyptic Cajun Turkey Burger

Classy Garden Burger

Mediterranean Citizens' Burgers

Squeaky Bacon Burger

Portabelly Burger

The USA Burger

Pimento Cheese Burger

Southwestern Burger Wraps

Stuffed Burgers & Golden–fried Onions

The Sloppy Joe

Jalapeño Chili Cheeseburgers

Seattle Salmon Burger

Onion & Mushroom Lucy

Pizza Burgers

Roman BBQ Sliders

Formal Tuna

Burgers, Beetroot, & Egg

Albino Burger

Nachos & Black Bean Burgers

Polynesian Burgers

Oh, Burger! (No Bun Intended)

Cheesy Roasted Garlic Burgers

Shrimp Burgers

Eggplant Parmesan Burgers

Pepper Burger with Mushroom–Merlot Gravy

Veggie Burger with Cheese

Philly Cheesesteak Burger

Relish the All–American Burger

Classic Veal Burgers

Berry Peachy Turkey

Montreal Tuna Burger

Potato Mini's

Caribbean Chicken Burger

Creole-styled Meat-Free Burger

Asian Chicken Burger

Blue Stuffed Burgers with Onion & Spinach

Home On the Range

Juicy Lucy Burger

Blue Vidalia Burgers

Chicken BBQ Burger

Thai Turkey Burgers

Salad Blues

Caramelized Onion Turkey Burger

Introduction

What is a Burger?

A universal favorite consisting of a roundish meat patty in a roundish bun.

Burgers can be served at road-side stalls or in high-class restaurants: literally anywhere, any time and in any form, too.

Fancy a deconstructed burger? How about to the point where its bun part is entirely absent and replaced by a lettuce leaf, no? …not quite your thing? Maybe the Asian version will interest you instead? Still no bun, but there is a square, pressed and grilled rice "burger" that is gluten free for sure.

Don't forget the vegetable activists who have redefined the word, "patty" to include all kinds of crazy and wonderful ingredients. Thanks to them, you can now find tasty stuff made from beans, tofu or other legumes.

Much like the humble sandwich, the variations are endless and the concept is often interpreted with much liberty. Wherever it's gone, the burger has been adapted to suit the local cuisine. Next time you pop over to India for a quick tea-run, try out the "Maharaja Mac" that replaces the famous Mickey D's Big Mac.

Then stop at a spot in Nevada known as the Heart Attack Grill. From among other disturbing offerings on the menu, you can pick out an "octuple"-bypass burger. Needless to say, the waitresses are all dressed in nurse's uniform. People that weigh over 350 pounds can even eat for free, all because these are burgers "worth dying for". Apparently, honesty really does pay; they have not spent a cent on advertising….

If you prefer a more studious approach to food, Sergey Brin, a co-founder of Google, funded $330,000 to research a "cowless" burger made entirely of lab-grown, bovine stem cells. It was eaten at a news conference in London in 2013 and reportedly tasted much like, well, a burger.

The History of the Burger

Historically, though, no one really knows where the idea of a hamburger came from. Some say the word is related to the place, Hamburg, in much the same way as a Frankfurter or Vienna is named after its birthplace. There are, however, some written documents that mention burgers way back in the 1800's.

Wait. 1800's?

That would look like a sepia man sporting coat tails, pantaloons and a top hat. Might he perhaps be checking to see if anyone saw him lick the sauce off his fingers? He would certainly not want dirty his fob watch before dinner...

Tips for Cooking Burgers

Speaking of which, there is no one right way to rustle up a burger meal. If we are talking about the traditional beef patty in a bun, then here are four ways to get the job done:

- Fry it – Use a cast iron pan over a medium heat. Cooking time will vary depending on the size of the patty, but the rules for cooking steak can be loosely followed. Make sure to let the meat rest a few minutes before serving too.

- Grill it – Using an open fire or a gas grill. Again, using medium heat. You will know the coals are good to go when they are all greyed over but still hot enough to burn you if for some reason you held your hand an inch away for more than two seconds.

- Broil it – The cheat version of a charcoal fire. You can use a toaster oven or a regular old oven-oven, as long as the patties are fairly close to the heat source.

- Steam it – Yup, this is a valid cooking method. It hasn't really caught on outside Connecticut, but can make a really juicy and moist variation to the regular deal. You can use empty tuna cans (cleaned – of course) and steam on medium-high for about 15-20 minutes.

Toppings, trimmings, sides and sauces are limited only by imagination; and depending on your GPS coordinates, you may find your burger is expected to have a side of fries, beans, maize porridge, Brussel sprouts, fruit, salad, coleslaw or even seafood!

So when you plan your next burger meal at home, don't be shy to experiment with all kinds of crazy combos. After all, if it has cheese on it, what could possibly go wrong?

Recipes

Mù Xū Pork Styled Burger

Mù Xū pork, pronounced "Moo shu" is often times served with hoisin sauce & "Báo B ĭ ng" or "Mandarin pancakes". Fairly recently, many USA Chinese restaurants have been using locally available (thicker & more brittle) Mexican–style tortillas.

Serves: 6
Time to Prepare: 15 min

Ingredients

Sauce:

* 6 Tbsp Light Mayo
* 2 Tbsp Hoisin Sauce (aka Black sauce or seafood sauce)

Mù Xū Pork Burger:

* 1¼ lb Ground Pork
* 4 oz Mushrooms, Finely Chopped (Preferably cremini)
* 2 Scallions, Trimmed & Cut into 1–2" Segments
* 1 Tbsp Soy Sauce
* 2 Tsp Ground Ginger

Serving:

* 6 Smallish Flour Tortillas (If you can't find "báo b ĭ ng" pancakes)
* 1 cup of Loosely Packed Rocket (Arugula)
* ½ cup Thinly Sliced Radishes

Directions

Get your coals ready (or your griller) to a medium heat. Grease a grill rack & have at the ready.

Sauce:

* Stir together the mayo & half the hoisin sauce (1 Tbsp). Pop it in the fridge & keep it there until you need it.

Burgers:

- Mix up the pork & the rest of the burger ingredients (mushrooms, scallions, soy sauce & ginger) with the remaining tablespoon of hoisin sauce. Roll into 6 balls & flatten them to look like patties.

To cook:

- Grill for 3 minutes per side. You want an internal temp of 160°F for them to be ready. Pop them on a plate & keep them warm.

Now it's serving time:

- Plop one Tbsp on the mayo–hoisin mix onto a tortilla & spread it lightly. Add the burger patty & the rocket/arugula & fan out some radish slices on top. Now fold the meal up into a handy little parcel of joy. And yumminess. Repeat x 6.

Vegetarian Chipotle Burger

Make a burger out of mashed black beans, rice, corn chips & kernels. Adjust the amount of spiciness to suit your/your family's preferences.

Serves: 8
Time to Prepare: 45 min

Ingredients

Patties:

- 2 Cans Black Beans, Rinsed (15 oz)
- 1 Can of Whole Kernel Corn, Drained (14 oz)
- 2 cups Corn Chips. Once Finely Crushed (Roughly 1 cup)
- 1 cup Brown Rice (Already cooked)
- ½ Small Red Onion, Chopped Finely (½ cup)
- ½ cup Chunky Salsa
- 2–3 Tsp Minced Chipotle Peppers
- 1 Tsp Cumin
- 2 Cloves Garlic, Finely Chopped

To Serve:

- 2 Tbsp Oil
- 8 Corn/Wheat Tortillas, Heated
- Some More Chunky Salsa
- Radishes, Sliced Finely
- Green Cabbage, Finely Shredded
- Fresh Cilantro
- Queso Fresco Cheese, Crumbled Up
- Avocado Pear Slices

Directions

The patties:

- Mash half the beans up (can use a food processor but not a blender: you want mash, not mush), toss into a large bowl & then mix the other half, followed by the corn & chips, rice, the onion, ½ cup of salsa, chipotle peppers, & the spices: cumin & garlic.

- Shape into 8 patties (roughly ¾" thick), cover & pop in the fridge for an hour before cooking. You could also freeze them for 3–4 hrs to make sure they are nice n firm. If you forget them in the freezer, that's ok… they can stay there in an airtight container for up to a month. Cook straight from frozen as below.

To cook:

- Brush both sides of the patty with oil & put them on the grill pan you intend to use.

- Charcoal grill: put the pan directly over medium coal until browned (8–10 min). As for steak, the rule of turning only once applies.

- Gas grill: preheat & bring heat down to med–hot. Grill as above – except you will want to cover the patties lightly with a sheet of foil.

To serve:

- Serve the burgers on tortillas of your choice. Top with the remaining ingredients.

Western Roasted Red Burger

This West Coast inspired recipe has the most divine red pepper spread. Make a double batch & use the extra on sandwiches tomorrow…

Serves: 4
Time to Prepare: 30 min

Ingredients

Onion Rings:

- 2 Med–sized Red Onions, Thickly Sliced
- Olive Oil for Brushing, Cooking, Etc

Red Spread:

- 1 Med–sized Sweet Red Pepper
- 12 Whole Almonds, Toasted
- ¼ cup Mayonnaise
- 2 Tsp Spicy Mustard
- 1 Clove of Garlic Clove
- ½ Tsp Salt
- A Dash of Black Pepper

Patties:

- 1½ lb Ground Chuck
- 1½ Tsp Salt
- 1 Tsp Black Pepper
- 4 Hamburger Rolls
- 4 Iceberg Lettuce Leaves

Directions

Prep:

- Heat the grill to around 400°F & then drop to med–hot.

The peppers:

- Grill the red peppers directly over the heat until black, keeping the lid shut for most of the time to preserve the heat build–up. Pop the peppers into a bowl & cover with cling film so that they can steam. This will loosen the skin so you can peel them when you take the seeds & stems out. Chop them roughly.

The onions:

- Brush them with oil on both sides & grill them as you did the red peppers. Not quite until black, but they must have pretty grill marks on them – you need them to be caramelized (10 min). When they are ready, pop them onto a chopping board & divide into two piles.

- Pile #1 needs to be chopped finely – it is going with the patty mix.

- Pile #2 will be reserved for serving.

The almonds & stuff:

- Toast them in a med–hot pan/skillet for around 4 minutes, stirring often. Once you are satisfied, pop them into a food processor with the peppers, mayo, mustard, garlic, salt, & pepper. Process until you have a nice smooth paste.

Time to patty:

- Increase the grill's temp to high (500°F), or if you happen to be doing an authentic outdoor fire, add additional coals to get the heat you need.

- Mix the meat, chopped onions, & seasoning in a nice big bowl. Divide the mix into 4 & shape into ¾" thick patties. Make a depression roughly 1" wide in the center of each one, so that the center is now only ½" thick.

...and cook:

- Keep the lid of the grill closed as much as possible. Cook for 10 min, turning once (they will be easier to lift off when they are ready to be flipped)

- Don't forget to toast the buns during the last minute of cooling. You only need a few seconds to warm them.

Assembly:

- Spread the red spread on the buns, pop the burger in the middle, with lettuce & the remaining half of the grilled onions that you set aside.

- Enjoy!

Burgers & Mexican Yam Slaw

The tasty Mexican yam bean or turnip is otherwise known as jicama, which, incidentally is also the same plant used to make insect poison. Only the tuberous root may be eaten. Who figured that out, perhaps?

Serves: 6
Time to Prepare: 30 min

Ingredients

Slaw:

* 1 Chipotle Pepper in Adobo Sauce
* ¼ oup Freshly Squeezed Lime Juice
* ½ Tsp Salt
* ⅓ cup Chopped Cilantro
* ¼ cup Sour Cream
* 2 Tbsp Mayo
* 2 cups Shredded Peeled Jicama

Patties:

* ¼ cup Fire–roasted Chunky Salsa (Comes in a bottle)
* 1 Clove Garlic, Finely Chopped
* 2 Tsp Chili Powder
* Another ½ Tsp Salt
* ¼ Tsp Ground Black Pepper
* 1½ lb Ground Beef
* ½ cup Black Beans (Canned), Rinsed

Serve:

* 6 Round Rolls, Cut Open & Toasted Just Right

Directions

Prep:

* Medium coals for a charcoal grill. For a gas grill, you need to pre–heat it & then set the temperature to med–high.

For the slaw:

- Put the chipotle pepper & lime juice with ½ Tsp of salt into a food processor. Whizz until nice & smooth. Now stir this mixture in with the cilantro, sour cream & mayo. Toss the shredded jicama in. Cover the bowl & set to one side for later.

Patties:

- Mix up the salsa, chili powder, ½ Tsp of salt, garlic & ground black pepper. Then mix in the meat & beans. Divide the mixture into 6 & shape into patties: ½" thick.

Cook:

- Grill the burger patties, on a lightly oiled rack, directly over the heat (if using gas: cover) until the internal temp is 160°F (10–14 min). Turn once halfway.

Serve:

- Open the roll up & place the patty on the one side & the slaw on the other.

Apple Bacon Burger

Apple & pork have been "bff" for centuries. Even in medieval times…

Serves: 4
Time to Prepare: 30 min

Ingredients

Burgers:

- ½ lb Italian Sausages
- ½ lb Ground Beef
- 1 Smallish Green Apple (Need 2 in total for this recipe)

Sauce:

- 2 Tbsp Mayo
- 1 Tbsp Mustard (Dijon)
- 1 Tsp Honey

To Serve:

- A Second Smallish Green Apple
- 4 Kaiser Rolls, Cut Open with the Faces Toasted
- 8 Slices Crispy Bacon

Directions

Prep:

- Get the bacon crispy & drain on paper towels. You can do this either under the broiler or in a pan on the stove – but be mindful to use med–high heat only!.

Make the patties:

- Now core & chop one of the apples into little bits so it can be mixed with the sausages & ground beef. Divide the mix into 4 balls & pat down until they are roughly ½" thick.

- Grill over coals or on a gas grill (med–high) until there is no more pink (4–5 min/side).

The sauce:

- While that is on the go, grab a bowl & mix together the mayo, mustard, & honey (use organic, raw honey if at all possible).

Last of all:

- Core the remaining apple & slice to whatever thickness suits your fancy.

…and serve:

- Bring the flavors together in a toasted Kaiser roll by layering the apples, patties & bacon inside. Then finish it off with a generous blob of the mustard–mayo mixture before closing the roll.

Smoky Southern–Style Burger

Tasty & smoky. Serve this with a side of beans, pickles & coleslaw. Make sure you have 2 cups of hickory wood chips handy for making this one extra special.

Serves: 6
Time to Prepare: 60 min

Ingredients

Burgers:

- 12 Slices Bacon (More if you like bacon)
- 2 lbs Ground Beef
- 2 Eggs, Lightly Beaten with a Fork
- 1 Tiny Sweet Onion, Finely Sliced (¼ cup)
- 1 Small Sweet Green Pepper, Finely Chopped (¼ cup)
- 1 Tsp Pepper
- ½ Tsp Salt (Try herbal or seasoned salt instead)
- ½ Tsp Dried Sage
- ¼ cup Barbecue Sauce
- 8 Hamburger Buns, Cut Open & Toasted if You Like

To Serve:

- Sliced Onions
- Barbecue Sauce
- Pickles
- Barbecue Beans
- Coleslaw

Directions

Prep:

- Cover the wood chips in water & soak them for at least an hour. Then drain them & set aside for later.

- Prepare the gas grill for indirect grilling. The temperature above the drip pan must be med–high. Add the wood to the grill as directed on its bag.

Burgers:

- Fry/broil or grill the bacon at a medium heat until crispy. Drain on paper towels & leave them until they are cool enough to crumble. Note: Only tiny test tastes are allowed.

- If possible, combine the full amount of bacon with the meat, eggs, onion, sweet pepper, seasoning & sage. Shape into 6 patties, get them about 1″ thick.

Cook:

- Oil the grill rack & place it over a drip pan. Pop the patties on & cook them (turning once) until the internal temp is 160°F (18–20 min), but be sure not to forget to brush them with barbecue sauce in the final 5 minutes.

To serve:

- Serve the burgers on buns, along with onions & extra barbecue sauce if you like. Serve with a side of pickle mix, barbecue beans, & coleslaw.

George-on-Diet Burger

Here is a version of a burger that is low fat & uses no meat

Serves: 4
Time to Prepare: 15 min

Ingredients

* 10 oz Frozen Soy Burgers
* 3 Tbsp Vegetable Soup/Broth/Stock
* 1 x 8 oz Can Pineapple Slices
* ½ Red Onion, Sliced
* 4 Whole-wheat Buns, Cut Open
* 4 Slices Fat-free Cheese (Processed or swiss)
* 1 Tbsp Fat-free Thousand Island Dressing
* 4 Lettuce Leaves

Directions

Charcoal grill:

* Cook directly over medium coals for 4 minutes per side, brushing with the broth to prevent drying out. Grill the pineapple & onion slices in the last 3 minutes; turning once.

* In the very last minute, grill the buns (inside parts facing down).

Gas grill:

* Preheat on high & reduce to med-hot. Position the meat on a rack over the heat & close the grill. Cook as for charcoal.

To serve:

* Assemble the burgers on the toasted buns, top with pineapple, onion, cheese, dressing & lettuce.

Apocalyptic Cajun Turkey Burger

Technically not a burger, but if you were in the middle of cooking one when the excitement went down, this is how it might end up. But that wouldn't really matter, I guess. You would be in too much of a hurry to notice how amazing it tastes… pity. Try it tonight anyway!

Serves: 5
Time to Prepare: 25 min

Ingredients

Hamburger Meat:

- 1 lb Ground Turkey
- 1 Small Red Bell Pepper, Chopped (½ cup)
- 2 Tsp Cajun Seasoning

Other Hamburger Ingredients:

- 2 cups Water (Hot)
- 1 cup of Milk
- 1 Box Cheeseburger & Macaroni Hamburger Helper or Similar
- 4 oz Grated Pepper Jack Cheese (1 cup)

Directions

Fry:

- Stir–fry the turkey, bell pepper & seasoning over med–high heat until the meat is no longer pink. Drain any excess liquid off.

Now add some liquid:

- Mix in the hot water, milk & pouch contents from the Hamburger Helper (or similar). Bring to the boil, & simmer (covered), stirring now & then until the pasta is tender (15 min)

To serve:

- Sprinkle cheese over the top & enjoy!

Classy Garden Burger

Cook these on an open fire for a full smoky flavor. Notes of freshly ground black pepper & fresh thyme. Top with blue cheese, rocket, summer squash, red onion & pickles.

Serves: 4
Time to Prepare: 20 min

Ingredients

Dressing:

- 2 Tbsp Oil
- 2 Tbsp Wine Vinegar (Red)
- 1 Tsp Freshly Chopped Thyme
- ¼ Tsp Coarsely Ground Black Pepper

Burger:

- 1 lb Ground Beef
- ¼ Tsp Salt
- ¼ Tsp Pepper

Toppings:

- 2 Med–sized Summer Squashes, Cut ¼–½" Slices Lengthways
- 2–4 oz Blue Cheese Wedges
- Rocket (aka Arugula); Lettuce Will Work Well Too

To Serve:

- 4 Round Buns, Opened & Toasted
- Tomato Slices
- Red Onion Slices
- Pickle Slices

Directions

Dressing:

- Mix the oil, vinegar, thyme & pepper together. You could throw it together in a sealable bottle & shake while singing "If you are happy & you know it". If you are feeling more serious, just mix with a teaspoon.

Patties:

- Grab a big bowl & mix the meat, ¼ Tsp salt & ¼ Tsp pepper. Make four equal balls of this mix & compress them to form ¾" patties.

Other prep:

- Brush the squash with some of the dressing & set aside

To cook:

- Charcoal grill: get coals to med–hot. Grill on a rack directly over the coals until done (14–18 min, 160°F). Turn only once. At the halfway point in cooking the patties, add the squash to the grill. Turn once only & cook until tender.

- Gas grill: Preheat, reduce to med–hot & grill as above (cook covered).

Serving time:

- Pop the meat into the buns & drizzle some dressing over the cut face of the top half of the bun. Top with the topping things & serve.

Mediterranean Citizens' Burgers

Here are three tasty variations of the classic patty in a bun from the folk living in the Mediterranean neighborhood. Trivia for the day: "burger" translates to "citizen" in Dutch.

Serves: 4
Time to Prepare: 20 min

Ingredients

- 1½ lb Ground Meat (Any kind)
- Garlic & Herb Salt
- Freshly Ground Pepper
- One of the Three Fillings Below

#1: Mediterranean (Mix All Ingredients):

- ¼ cup Mayo
- ¼ cup Parmesan (Freshly grated is best)
- 2 Tbsp Thin Slices of Green Onion
- 2 Tbsp Skinny Sliced Olives (Ripe, no pits)

#2: La España (Mix All Ingredients):

- 2 Tbsp Finely Sliced Tomato
- 2 Tbsp Cleaned & Finely Chopped Jalapeños
- 2 Tbsp Minced (Fresh) Cilantro
- 2 Tbsp Thinly Sliced Green Onion

- #3: Greecey Burger (Mix All Ingredients, Chill for 30 Min):

- ¼ cup Chopped Tomato
- 1 oz Crumbled Feta
- 2 Tsp Sliced Red Onion (Finely sliced)
- 2 Tsp Finely Sliced Olives (Ripe, no pits)
- ¼ Tsp Wine Vinegar (Red)
- ¼ Tsp Olive Oil
- A Dash of Dried Oregano

Directions

You are going to make 4 "patty–sandwiches", so divide meat into 8 equal portions. Flatten them out to roughly 4" wide.

Pop 2 Tbsp of the chosen filling into the center & spread it to within ½ an inch of the edge.

Place the "tops" on & gently press the edges together to seal. Season to taste with garlic salt & pepper.

For an authentic charcoal grill:

- Cook directly over med–hot coals & turn only once. Total cook time: 14–18 min or until internal temp is 160°F.

If using gas:

- Preheat & set heat to medium. Cover & grill as per charcoal method

Squeaky Bacon Burger

Cheese curd, a.k.a. squeaky cheese can lose a bit of its fresh squeak if kept refrigerated. Leaving it at room temp can help preserve that. It has a mild flavor & can be easily substituted with string cheese, a mozzarella/cheddar hybrid.

Serves: 4
Time to Prepare: 20 min

Ingredients

The Burger:

- 4 Thick Bacon Slices
- ¼ cup Packed Raw Brown Sugar
- 2 lbs Ground Chuck or Sirloin
- ¾ cup Cheese Curds (or String Cheese), Chopped
- Salt & Pepper

To Serve:

- 4 Hamburger Buns
- Toppings of Your Choice (Slices of tomato/onion & lettuce)

Directions

Prep:

- Heat oven to 450°F.

- Grab a (unheated) broiler pan & lay the slices of bacon out. Sprinkle each one with brown sugar & pop into the oven.

- Cook until nice & crisp (10 min). When it's coolish, chop it into bits & set aside, well out of anyone's reach.

Patties:

- Now take the meat & divide it into 8 balls. Bop them down until you have a roughly ¾" high x 4" round disk. Set four aside.

- Divide the bacon bits & cheese into 4 portions & match each one to its burger. Eyeball a ½" rim around each patty & make sure there is no bacon or cheese escaping the perimeter of this "clear zone".

- Put the other for patties on top as lids & pinch the edges closed. Leave in the fridge for an hour to firm up.

Time to cook:

- Bring the patties out & season them with salt & pepper.

- Charcoal: Oil a rack & cook over med–hot coals for 10 minutes. Turn carefully & grill for another 10–12 min (160°F). Toast the cut faces of the buns in the last minute or so.

- Gas: The same, except put the grill on full blast to heat the space & then set to med–hot. Cover the patties.

To serve:

- Put the burger on a bun with tomatoes, onion, lettuce & any other sauces you fancy. Just be aware that the cheese in the patty will be hot & may burn you.

Portabelly Burger

A meatless burger like no other. Yummy. No description needed..

Serves: 4
Time to Prepare: 30 min

Ingredients

Burger Bits:

- 1 Clove Garlic, Minced to the Point Where It is Mashable
- ½ Tsp Salt
- Some Olive Oil (2 Tbsp in all)
- 4 Portobello Mushrooms (Preferably, because of their size)
- 4 Chunky Slices of Country–style Sourdough Bread, Cut in Half & Lightly Toasted

Salady Bits:

- ½ cup Sliced Roasted Red Peppers
- 1 Small Tomato, Chopped (½ cup)
- 1 oz Crumbled Feta Cheese (¼ cup)
- 2 Tbsp Chopped Olives
- 1 Tbsp Wine Vinegar (Red)
- ½ Tsp Oregano
- 2 cups Mixed Baby Salad Greens

Directions

Prep:

- Get the grill going on high & then drop the temperature to med–hot.

Roast the red (if necessary):

- Lay the pepper on the open grill & give it ¼ of a turn every few minutes or so. You need to get them charred & a little "floppy" (15–20 min)

Mushroom burger:

- Mash garlic & salt with the side of a knife until it's nice & smooth. Mix this paste with 1 Tbsp of the oil in a dish. Lightly brush the oil mixture over portobellos & then on one side of each slice of bread.

Red pepper mix:

- Grab a bowl & let the roasted red peppers, the tomato, feta, olives, vinegar, oregano & the remaining oil become acquainted with each other. Toss the baby greens in.

Cook:

- Grill the mushroom until just tender (don't overcook); 4 min/side.

- Crisp the bread up a bit on the grill; 1 min/side.

Now assemble:

- Lay the mushrooms on four of the slices (top side down) & spoon the red pepper salad over the top & perch the remaining bread at the side.

The USA Burger

An All–American burger that will put a smile on your face & sauce on your fingers!

Serves: 4
Time to Prepare: 10 min

Ingredients

Sauce:

- 2 Tbsp Ketchup
- 1 Tbsp Worcestershire Sauce
- 1 Tbsp Your Favorite Steak Sauce
- 1 Tsp Sugar
- A Tiny Splash of Oil
- 1 Tsp Vinegar
- 1 Clove of Garlic, Minced (Pre–minced ½ Tsp)
- A Few Dashes of Hot Pepper Sauce

Burgers:

- 1 lb Ground Beef
- ¼ Tsp Salt
- ¼ Tsp Black Pepper

To Serve:

- 4 Hamburger Buns, Cut in Half & Toasted
- Fresh Salsa (Bottled if you are running low on time)
- Various Toppers Like Lettuce/Cornichons/Radish Halves/Cucumber Slices

Fresh Salsa:

- Mix All Ingredients & Chill for Later.
- 1 cup Chopped Red & Yellow Tomatoes (Only the flesh)
- 3 Tbsp Finely Sliced Red Onion
- 2 Tbsp Freshly Chopped Cilantro
- 1 Finely Chopped, Fresh Serrano Chili (With or without Seeds)
- 1 Tbsp Freshly Squeezed Lime Juice
- 1 Tsp Pure Honey

Directions

Prep:

- Get your gas/charcoal grill to a med–high heat.

For sauce:

- In a little pot, combine the ketchup, Worcestershire sauce, steak sauce, & sugar, tiny splash of oil, vinegar, garlic, & hot sauce. Bring up to the boil & lower the heat. Simmer, uncovered, for 5 minutes. Keep one side for later use.

Burgers:

- Next, mix you meat & seasoning together & shape into 4 patties: ¾″ thick.

To cook

- Place patties on an oiled grill rack (directly above the heat) & grill until internal temperature is 160°F (14–18 min). Turn once only & baste often with sauce.

To serve:

- Serve burgers on buns topped with salsa & whatever else you fancy, like lettuce, gherkins, radish halves, & cucumber slices.

Pimento Cheese Burger

Home is where the cheese is

Serves: 6
Time to Prepare: 25 min

Ingredients

- 1 lb Ground Sirloin
- 1 lb Ground Chuck
- 1½ Tsp Salt
- ½ Tsp Pepper
- 6 Hamburger Buns
- Pimento Cheese As Below

Pimento Cheese:

- 1 Shallot, Very Finely Sliced & Chopped & Diced
- 1 x 8 oz Block Sharp Cheddar, Grated
- ½–⅓ cup Regular Mayonnaise
- 2 oz Pimentos (From a jar; can substitute for sweet red pepper)
- Coarse Ground Black Pepper to Taste

Directions

Prep:

- Get your coals going; you will need a med–hot cooking space. If using gas, preheat & then drop the heat to medium.

Burgers:

- Mix the meat(s) together with salt & pepper. Divide into six patties (don't forget to make the indent in the center so that cooking all the way through becomes easier.

Cook & serve:

- Brush with olive oil & place directly over the heat. Grill until they look tasty, turning once at the halfway point (10–12 min). When you take them off the grill, immediately top them with a spoon of Pimento Cheese & pop into the buns.

Pimiento Cheese:

- Combine the shallot & cheese. Add the mayo & stir until mixture begins to holds together. Now stir in the pimentos. Use a little of the liquid from the jar for extra flavor. Season & leave in the fridge until you need it.

Southwestern Burger Wraps

Oblong patties in a wrap. With cheese, meat & vegetables!

Serves: 4
Time to Prepare: 25 min

Ingredients

The Burgers:

- 12 oz Ground Beef
- 1 cup Refried Beans
- ½ cup Freshly Chopped Cilantro
- 1 Tbsp Sliced Jalapeños (Pickled)
- Guacamole
- 1 Avocado
- ½ cup Salsa
- A Dash of Powdered Garlic

Assembly:

- Romaine Lettuce Leaf Bits (±2 cups)
- ½ cup Shredded (Pepper Jack) Cheese
- 1 Lime, Cut in 4
- 4 Whole–wheat Tortillas, Warmed (Wrap in lightly dampened paper towels & microwave on high for 30 seconds)

Directions

Position an oven rack in the top third of your oven & get the element heating. Get the broiler pan ready & greased so long.

Make the patties:

- Mix the burger ingredients gently (ground beef, beans, cilantro & pickles chili) & shape them into four oblong patties (roughly 5x2")

Broil the patties:

- Broil until golden; your meat thermometer should read 165°F (12–14 min)

Guac:

- Mash the avocado, salsa & garlic powder together in a bowl. You can serve this with the meal & let everyone assemble their own burger/tortilla inventions if you like.

...and finally:

- Spread each tortilla with guacamole, sprinkle with cheese & some lettuce. Now pop the burger on top of that & it's a wrap. Serve fresh with a lime wedge.

Stuffed Burgers & Golden-fried Onions

This is an upgrade on the classic burger & is deceptively simple. These can be made the night before, wrapped in cling wrap & stored in the fridge. Make sure they are back at room temperature before you grill them.

Serves: 4
Time to Prepare: 25 min

Ingredients

Relish:

- 3 Small Onions, Sliced (3 cups)
- 4 Tsp Olive Oil
- ¼ Tsp Salt
- ¼ Tsp Freshly Ground Pepper

Patties:

- 1 lb Ground Beef
- 2 Tbsp Worcestershire Sauce
- ½ Tsp Freshly Ground Pepper
- 2 Cloves Garlic, Finely Chopped/Minced
- 3 oz Grated Swiss Cheese (¾ cup)

To Serve:

- 1 Loaf French Bread (4 x ¾" Thick diagonal slices)
- 1 Tbsp Olive Oil for Brushing

Directions

Use 4 Tsp oil to fry the onion over a medium heat until golden (10 min). Mix in salt & ¼ Tsp pepper & cover the pan to keep warm.

While the onions are doing their thing, mix the meat, garlic, Worcestershire sauce & ½ Tsp freshly ground pepper. Divide into 8 balls & shape each one into a patty (±4" wide). Spread the cheese between 4 of them & then close the "patty sandwich" with the remaining 4. Press the edges together to seal them.

Charcoal grill:

- Cook directly over medium coals – turning once only – until done for (14–18 min; 160°F)

Broiler:

* Pop the patties on the rack of a broiler pan. Leave them to cook 3–4″ below the heat. Cook as above for charcoal directions.

Brush the French bread slices lightly with olive oil & grill/broil until toasted (the last 2–3 minutes of cooking).

Serve with a patty on each & top with onion relish.

The Sloppy Joe

This is a delicious 4–quart slow cooker recipe. Sloppy Joes originated in the USA in the roaring 20's & has been a classic favorite ever since. This jazzed up version will make you happy. Dancing is also permitted.

Serves: 16
Time to Prepare: 40 min

Ingredients

Slow Cook:

- 3 lbs Ground Beef/Pork
- 2 Onions, Chopped (2 cups)
- 4 Cloves Garlic, Finely Chopped
- 2½ cups Sliced Sweet Red Peppers
- 4 Stalks of Celery, Chopped (2 cups)
- 1 Can of Beer (12 oz)
- 2 Tbsp Mustard
- 4 Tsp Chili Powder
- 2 Tsp Unrefined Apple Cider Vinegar
- Dash Hot Pepper Sauce
- 1 cup Ketchup
- 2 Tbsp Molasses

To Serve:

- 16 Round Rolls, Cut Open & Toasted
- Assorted Toppers: Pickle Slices/Pickled Peppers, Etc.

Directions

Prep:

- Fry up the meat, onions & garlic over a medium heat until the onions are tender & meat is brown. Don't over–cook. Drain off any excess fat.

Cook:

- Grab your slow cooker & pop the meat mix in along with the sweet peppers, beer, sliced up celery, molasses, ketchup & mustard, chili powder, vinegar, & lastly, hot sauce.

- Cover & cook on low for 6–8 hours. If you are in a hurry, use the high setting for 3–4 hours.

Serve:

- To serve, spoon meat over the toasted buns' bottom halves. Add any toppings that make you happy & close the buns. Enjoy!

Jalapeño Chili Cheeseburgers

Lime, jalapeños, cheese, & hickory... This is a must–try for any burger enthusiast. Just ensure you have 2 cups of hickory chips handy.

Serves: 8
Time to Prepare: 25 min

Ingredients

Burgers:

* ⅓ cup Finely Chopped Green Onions (Scallions)
* 3 Tbsp Plain Yogurt
* 1–4 Tbsp Finely Chopped & De–seeded Jalapeños
* ½ Tsp Salt
* ½ Tsp Black Pepper
* 2 lbs Ground Beef
* 6 x 1 oz Slices of Cheese (Monterey jack with jalapeño peppers)

Serve:

* 8 Kaiser Rolls, Cut Open & Toasted Lightly
* 8 Lettuce Leaves
* Sliced Tomato
* Lime Mayonnaise (Mix ⅓ cup mayo with ½ Tsp lime zest, 1 Tsp lime juice & 1 Tsp dijon mustard – cover & chill for later)

Directions

Prep:

* Soak the hickory chips in water for an hour.

* Heat your grill up to medium. Preheat your coals.

Burgers:

* Mix the scallions, yogurt, jalapeños & seasoning, then mix the meat in. Divide the mixture into 8 & shape into patties: ¾" thick. Make a little depression in the middle of each one.

Cook:

- Arrange preheated coals in a covered grill around a drip pan. Drain the wood chips & spread on the coals.

- Grill the burgers on the rack above drip pan, keeping the lid closed. Cook, turning once, until the internal temperature of the meat is 165°F (20–24 min). Put a piece of cheese on each patty for the last 2 min.

Serve:

- Serve on round rolls with lettuce, tomato, & your home–made lime mayonnaise.

Seattle Salmon Burger

Salmon has a very distinctive & delicate flavor. This is a beautiful & elegant recipe that showcases exactly that.

Serves: 4
Time to Prepare: 30 min

Ingredients

Salmon Patty:

- 1 lb Salmon Fillet
- 4 Green Parts of Scallions, Sliced into 1" Segments
- 4 Garlic Cloves, Chopped Finely
- 2 Tbsp Freshly Grated Ginger
- 2 Tbsp Tamari (Darker & richer than regular soy sauce)
- ¼ cup Breadcrumbs
- 2 Tbsp Sesame Seeds
- Salt & Pepper to Taste
- 1 Tbsp Toasted Sesame Oil (Darker & richer flavor than untoasted)

To Serve:

- 4 Hamburger Rolls, Cut Open
- Lettuce
- Asian Sweet Chili Sauce or Peanut Sauce

Directions

Make the salmon patty:

- Acquire some good quality salmon, skin removed & thoroughly deboned. Cut it into chunks & put it in a food processor with the scallions, garlic, fresh ginger, tamari (or soy sauce as an alternative) & sesame oil. Pulse a few times until combined. Make sure the machine doesn't run, otherwise, you will land up with soup….

- Now pop this in a bowl & use your hands (hands & nails scrubbed clean, or use latex–free surgical gloves if mixing with your hands grosses you out) to incorporate the breadcrumbs & sesame seeds.

- Make four patties, roughly ¾" thick & put a slight indent in the center of each one. Season both sides generously with salt & pepper & pop into the fridge for at least 1 hour.

- If you are running short on time, you can put them in the freezer, but be careful that they don't solidify. You want them to be firm enough to hold themselves together when you cook them – not frozen solid.

Cooking time:

- Heat the grill full blast for 10 minutes or so, & then drop the setting to medium high. Make sure the grill racks are squeaky–clean & properly oiled if you intend to complete your mission with the patties intact.

- Brush both sides of the patties with oil (or a puff of cooking spray) & pop onto the waiting grill. Cook for 5 minutes, loosen with a spatula before attempting to turn them; cook on the other side for 4–5 min so they are just cooked through. Right at the end of the cooking process, pop the buns onto the grill to toast.

To serve:

- Arrange the burgers & buns on a plate with lettuce & your chosen sauce drizzled over the top.

Onion & Mushroom Lucy

This burger is similar to the Juicy Lucy in form, but with a different filling & added bacon. Mmmm..

Serves: 8
Time to Prepare: 50 min

Ingredients

Filling:

- 3 Medium Onions, Sliced (1½ cups)
- 8 oz Mushrooms, Sliced (3 cups)
- 1 Tbsp Oil
- 2 Tbsp Freshly Chopped Parsley

Patties:

- 2½ lbs Ground Beef
- ⅓ cup Worcestershire Sauce
- 4 Cloves Garlic, Finely Chopped
- 1½ Tsp Salt
- 1 Tsp Pepper
- 16 Skinny Strips of Bacon Plus More for "Testing" (1 lb)
- 8 Slices of Cheese

To Serve:

- 8 Hamburger Buns, Cut Open & Toasted
- Tomato Slices

Directions

Filling:

- Get the onions & mushrooms a fryin' in hot oil over a medium heat. Keep going until all the liquid has evaporated & they look tasty (15–20 min). Stir in the parsley & leave take off the heat to sit quietly on the side.

Now for the patties:

- Do not over mix, but combine the meat, W/sauce, garlic & seasoning. Divide this mix into 16 x 3½"–wide patties & spoon the filling onto half of them.

Make sure that you have at least ½" of edge to work with, otherwise you won't be able to seal them properly.

- Put the "lids" on the filled meat and pinch the edges closed. Wrap each patty in two strips of bacon (not essential – said no one ever) like a little gift & tuck the ends under the parcel.

To cook:

- Charcoal: Cook on a grill rack over a drip pan over med–hot coals. Cover & cook until er, cooked? Internal temp should register 160°F (25–30 min). Turn once.

- Gas: Preheat grill on high & drop the setting to med–high. Cover & grill on a rack over a drip pan, same as above.

- Top with the cheese that hopefully has not yet been snaffled by curious kitchen–loiterers. Cover & cook until cheese melts (1–2 min)

Serve:

- Serve on toasted buns with tomato slices & whatever other trimmings take your fancy.

Pizza Burgers

Ah, finally, you no longer have to choose which one you want… two for the price of one!

Serves: 4
Time to Prepare: 20 min

Ingredients

Burger Mix:

* 1 Egg, Lightly Beaten with a Fork
* ⅓ cup Canned Mushrooms, Drained & Sliced
* ¼ cup Seasoned Bread Crumbs
* 2 Tbsp Milk
* 1 Tsp Dried Italian Herb Mix
* ¼ Tsp Salt

Sauce:

* 1 Can Pizza Sauce (8 oz)
* ¼ cup Sliced Olives
* 1 lb Ground Pork

To Serve:

* 8 Man–sized Chunks of French Bread
* ¼ cup Mozzarella Cheese Grated (1 oz)

Directions

Prep:

* Build your charcoal grill & get the coals to a med–high heat.

* For gas, preheat at full blast & then set the temp to med–hot. Cover & grill as for charcoal.

Patties:

* Combine the beaten egg, mushrooms, bread crumbs, milk, seasoning, & salt. Mix in the meat & shape into four patties, ¾″ thick.

Cook:

- Grill until internal temp is 160°F (14–18 min), turning once at the halfway point. Toast the bread in the last few minutes of cooking the meat.

The sauce:

- Put the olives & pizza sauce in a little pot & cook until the olives are heated through.

To serve:

- Serve burgers between slices of bread with the pizza & olive sauce & sprinkle with a bit of cheese.

Roman BBQ Sliders

A slider is typically a small burger. This is ideal for a cocktail party.

Serves: 12
Time to Prepare: 15 min

Ingredients

* 3 lbs Ground Beef (Chuck works well)
* ¼ cup Your Favorite Steak Sauce
* Salt & Pepper
* 1 Bag Roma Tomatoes
* 1 Bunch Fresh Basil
* 24 Round Rolls
* Pesto Mayo Sauce (Mix ½ cup mayo with 2 Tbsp of basil pesto)
* Fresh Mozzarella Cheese, As Needed

Directions

Prep:

* Get your gas/charcoal fire to medium heat.

Burger:

* Grab a large bowl & add the meat, sauce & seasoning. Mix well. Shape the meat into 24 patties.

Cook:

* Brush the grill with oil & pop the burgers on. Cook for 4–6 min/side, depending on how well you want them done.

* Halve the buns & toast the cut side on the grill.

To serve:

* Spread pesto mayo on both sides of each bun & pop the patties in with a slice of cheese, tomato & a fresh leaf of basil.

Formal Tuna

Elegantly simple fish burgers with a little Thai to dress it up

Serves: 4
Time to Prepare: 10 min

Ingredients

The Burgers:

- ⅓ cup Olive Oil & Mayo Mix
- 2 Tsp Freshly Grated Ginger
- 2 Eggs (Lightly beaten)
- 1 cup Bread Crumbs – Japanese Style (aka Panko)
- 1 Tbsp Fish Sauce
- 2 Cans (5 oz) Albacore Tuna (Firmer texture & mild)
- ¼ cup Finely Sliced Celery
- ¼ cup Sliced Green Onions (or Scallions)
- 1 Tsp Sriracha Sauce

To Serve:

- 2 Smallish Ciabatta Rolls, in Half & Toasted
- ⅓ cup Pea Sprouts (Micro greens could also work)
- 2 Mini Sweet Peppers, Finely Sliced

Directions

Get the oven to 450°F.

Make the burger:

- Mix the mayo blend & ginger together & pop it in the fridge to chill out.

- Take 2 Tbsp of this mayo blend & mix it in with the flaked tuna & the rest of the ingredients. Leave this to sit around for 10 minutes for the flavor to combine.

- Wet your hands & "jiggle" the tuna mix into four ¾" patties.

- Oil a baking sheet & gently transfer the patties. Bake them until done (160°F), this should take 10 minutes.

Now the fun part:

- Grab that ginger–mayo you put aside in the fridge & spread it in the toast. Pop a patty onto each bun, top with the green bits & peppers of choice. Then perch the top half of the bun on.

Burgers, Beetroot, & Egg

This is a rather interesting combination. If you have leftover pickled beetroot from last night's dinner, you could use that… or from a jar of store–bought pickled beets. But that would be cheating, now, wouldn't it?

Serves: 4
Time to Prepare: 30 min

Ingredients

Beetroot:

- 2 Med–sized Beetroots
- ½ cup Sugar
- ½ cup Water
- ½ cup Wine Vinegar (White)
- 3 Strips Orange Peel
- 2½ Tsp Salt
- ½ Tsp Cracked Black Pepper

Patties:

- 1 lb Ground Beef Chuck
- 8 oz Ground Beef Sirloin
- ¼ Tsp Ground Black Pepper

To Serve:

- 4 Kaiser or Hamburger Rolls, Cut Open
- 2 Tsp Oil
- 4 Eggs
- 2 oz Soft Goat Cheese
- 4 Frilly Lettuce Leaves (Bibb lettuce)

Directions

Beetroot:

- In a large saucepan combine the beetroots & enough water to cover them. Bring the water to the boil & reduce the heat. Pop the lid on (you may need to perch it an angle to prevent spillage) & cook until tender (30 min).

- Drain & leave them to cool a bit. Then rub off the peels under running water (or use a knife to skin them).

- Now halve them lengthwise & julienne. Keep one side.

- Find a medium-sized pan (you will add the beetroot to it in a moment) & bring sugar, water, vinegar, orange peel, the cracked black pepper & only 2 Tsp of the salt to the simmer. Stir to dissolve the sugar. Once the sugar is dissolved, add the beetroot & remove from the heat.

- Leave the mix to stand for about half an hour for the flavors to combine. Drain & discard the liquid.

Burgers:

- While the beetroots do all their cooking & waiting etc., you may as well combine the meat(s) with the remaining salt & ¼ Tsp ground pepper. Shape into four ¾" thick patties.

Now cook the burgers:

- Charcoal grill: Grill on the rack of an uncovered grill directly over med–hot coals until the internal temp is 160°F (10–12 min), turning once halfway through.

- Gas: Cook as above, but covered.

- Once you take the patties off the grill, let them rest for 5 minutes. While you do this, you can pop the rolls onto the grill lack for a few minutes to toast them lightly. You are almost ready to serve.

Eggs:

- Break the eggs into a pan over a med–hot heat. Cover & cook of 2 minutes, then turn the heat off so that the eggs can cook in the trapped heat for another 2 minutes. The whites should be set & the yellows just cooked.

To serve:

- Spread the goat's cheese on the bottom (cut) side of each roll. To with lettuce leaves, the burgers, cooked beetroot strips, & the eggs. Pop the roll tops back on.

Albino Burger

This is an interesting & a rather different take on the traditional burger. Think of the little journey your taste buds will take when you bite into a sweet–spicy–savory burger with a hint of white wine. Oohlala. Garnish with some lettuce bits for color.

Serves: 4
Time to Prepare: 20 min

Ingredients

Pears:

- 1 Ripe Pear, Inedible Bits Removed & Thinly Sliced
- ½ cup Dry Wine (White)
- 1½ Tbsp Lemon Juice

Turkey Burger:

- 1 lb Ground Turkey Breast
- 2 Scallions/Green Onions, Minced
- ½–1 Tbsp Dijon Mustard
- 1 Tsp Lemon Zest
- 1½ Tsp Freshly Chopped Thyme
- ½ Tsp Salt
- ¼ Tsp Black Pepper

Other Cooking Ingredients:

- 1 Tbsp Oil
- 4 oz Sharp White Cheddar Cheese Grated (1 cup)

To Serve:

- 4 Tbsp Green Jalapeño Jam/Jelly/Preserve
- 4 Ciabatta Rolls, Sliced Open & Toasted

Directions

The pears:

- Get the pear slices, wine & lemon juice (and just enough water to cover them) to a boil in a med–sized pan. Then reduce the heat & simmer gently until the pears are softish (5 min). Carefully lift the slices out with a slotted spoon & put on a plate for later.

The turkey patty:

- While the pears are poaching away, make the patties. Combine the turkey & other patty ingredients (scallions, mustard, lemon zest, thyme, salt & pepper) together & shape into four patties

Time to cook:

- Get a large pan heating over a medium heat. Oil & fry the patties until no longer pink, turning once only. (8–10 min; 170°F).

- During the last minute or so of cooking, top each one with pear & cheese. Cover & cook until the cheese has melted.

Assembly:

- Don't forget to toast the buns. Then spread 1 Tbsp chili jam/jelly/preserve on the bottom half of each roll. Then pop the burger & pear concoction on top & close the bun.

Nachos & Black Bean Burgers

This time, we have a burger with nacho & salsa goodness. Prepare these patties the night before if you like.

Serves: 4
Time to Prepare: 25 min

Ingredients

Burger:

- 1 Can Black Beans (15 oz), Rinsed
- ½ cup Blue Corn Tortilla Chips, Finely Crushed
- ⅔ cup Salsa (Keep ⅓ aside for serving time)
- ½ cup Grated Cheddar
- 1 Large Egg, Lightly Beaten with a Fork
- 1 Scallion, Finely Sliced (White & green parts)
- ¼ Tsp Freshly Ground Black Pepper

To Serve:

- 4 Round Rolls
- A Splash or Two of Oil (2 Tsp if you really want to measure it)
- 4 Lettuce Leaves

Directions

Make the patties:

- Mash or pulse the beans in a food processor until chunky, don't worry if a few are whole still. Mix in the crushed chips, salsa, cheese, egg, chopped scallion & black pepper.

- Leave the mixture to rest for 10 minutes & then shape into 4 patties. Place patties on a plate, cover with plastic wrap & refrigerate at least 30 minutes or overnight.

To cook:

- When you are ready to cook, heat the oven to 350°F to warm the buns for 5 minutes.

- **Tip:** Mist the buns before putting them in. This will keep them from drying out.

- Meanwhile, heat your pan with 1 Tsp oil over medium heat. Pop the patties in the pan & cook until golden brown on one side (5 min). Add the remaining oil & flip them over to cook for yet another 5 min.

To serve:

- If you want to, you can serve them on buns. Otherwise, just serve them with salsa & lettuce.

Polynesian Burgers

Think of tropical beaches & pineapples. Now add some ground beef & a frying pan..

Serves: 6
Time to Prepare: 30 min

Ingredients

Burger:

- 1½ lb Ground Beef
- 1 x 8 oz Can Pineapple Slices (Keep the juice)
- 1 x 10½ oz Can Condensed French Onion Soup
- 2 Tsp Packed Brown Sugar
- 1 Tbsp Unrefined Apple Cider Vinegar

To Serve:

- 1 Loaf of French Bread Cut Diagonally into 6 Pieces

Directions

Divide the meat into 6 & pat the balls down to ½" thick.

Fry them over a med–high heat until well browned on both sides. Top each patty with a pineapple slice.

Combine the condensed soup, pineapple juice from the can, sugar, & vinegar in a bowl. Pour this into the pan with the patties in it & bring to the boil, then drop the heat setting to low. Keep it hot until the burgers are cooked through (5 min).

Split the French loaf pieces up & serve with the burgers & warm sauce. Enjoy!

Oh, Burger! (No Bun Intended)

For those of us who have issues & allergies, but still wish to retain a semblance of normality

Serves: 6
Time to Prepare: 20 min

Ingredients

- 2 lbs Ground Beef
- 8 oz Italian Sausage
- 3 oz Parmesan, Sliced into 1x¼" Portions
- ¼ cup 1" Slices of Roasted Sweet Peppers (±12 pieces)
- Salt & Pepper
- Lettuce Leaves for "Wrapping" Each Patty
- 6 Fresh Cherry Tomatoes

Directions

Grab a big bowl & roughly mix the meat–meat & sausage–meat with your hands. Shape into 12 even balls to make 6 "patty–sandwiches".

Tip: Spread out some wax paper & build your patties on it. This way they are easier to lift.

Bop each ball to form a roughly 4–4½" diameter patty. Sprinkle the Parmesan & sweet peppers on the 6 bottom halves, & then top each with its mate. Press together gently to seal the edges. Season with salt & pepper.

Charcoal grill:

- Surround a drip–pan with med–hot coals. Cover with a foil blanket & grill the patties on the rack over the pan until the center of each patty reads 160°F (18–22 min). If you want the burgers to look pretty, move them directly over the coals for the last 2–3 min of cooking. They will brown slightly.

Gas:

- Preheat on high & then drop the temp to medium. Place patties on a rack & close the grill. Cook as per charcoal instructions

To serve, place a patty between lettuce leaves & attach a cherry tomato to each one with a toothpick.

Cheesy Roasted Garlic Burgers

Roast some garlic yourself – it's dead easy. It goes beautifully with cheese & basil & is just yummy. A winner all round.

Serves: 6
Time to Prepare: 20 min

Ingredients

Roasted Garlic:

- 2 Garlic Bulbs
- 1 Tbsp Oil

Patties:

- ¾ cup Grated Parmesan (3 oz)
- 1 Small Onion, Finely Sliced (⅓ cup)
- ⅓ cup Oil–packed Dried Tomatoes, Snipped Up Finely
- ½ cup Freshly Chopped Basil
- ½ Tsp Black Pepper
- ¼ Tsp Salt
- 1½ lb Ground Beef
- 8 oz Italian Sausage
- 6 oz Mozzarella Cheese

To Serve:

- 6 Ciabatta/Round Rolls, Opened
- Olive Oil
- Baby Spinach Leaves
- Ripe Olives for Garnishing
- Olive Mayo (Mix ½ cup mayonnaise, 1 Tbsp freshly basil & 1–2 Tbsp olive tapenade)

Directions

Set the oven to heat at 400°F.

Roasted garlic:

- Chop the tips off the garlic bulbs (exposing the tops of the cloves) & remove the loose papery leaves. You will now make foil parcels with the bulbs in the middle: spread out the foil, put the bulbs cut side down & drizzle the lot with 1 Tbsp olive oil.

- Now wrap the foil up & over to make a package. Roast until the cloves are soft & starting to pull loose (30–35 min). When cool enough to handle, squish the cloves out & mash to form a paste.

The patties:

- Now add this tasty–smelling garlic together with the Parmesan, onion, dried tomatoes, basil, pepper, & salt. Mix lightly & then the meats can join the party. Again, mix very lightly & shape into 12 patties: ½" thick & 4" wide.

...and the filling:

- Slice up the mozzarella into 6 slices (½" wide). Top half the patties with cheese & then close the "sandwich" with the other 6 patties. Pinch the edges together to seal. You don't want cheese leaking out. Cheese is sacred.

Now cook:

- Charcoal grill: Place a drip pan in between some med–hot coals Cook the patties on a rack above the pan, but make sure that the temperature around the rack is also med–hot. Grill for 10 min, turn & grill until done (160°F), about 10 min.

- Gas grill: Preheat & lower heat to med–hot. Pop the patties onto a rack away from the heat & cover the grill. Cover & cook as per charcoal instructions.

...but don't forget the buns:

- Brush the insides with oil & get them toasting (over direct heat) during the last minute of cooking the meat. Assemble with leaves & olives & serve with a wooden skewer through the middle. Beware the cheese inside is really hot.

Shrimp Burgers

A seafood take on a hamburger. Simple & tasty.

Serves: 4
Time to Prepare: 10 min

Ingredients

- 2 Round Rolls for Crumbs (or Use bought ones: 1½ cups).
- 1¼ lb Cleaned Up Shrimp
- ⅓ cup Mayo
- 1 Tsp Salt
- ½ Tsp Pepper
- 2 Tbsp Butter

For Serving:

- 4 Hamburger Rolls
- 6 Lettuce Leaves (Iceberg)
- Tartar Sauce

Directions

Make crumbs out of the buns (using a food processor) or use the bought crumbs. Empty into a large dish.

Pulse the shrimp in the processor until fairly fine, but not mashed. Empty this into the bowl with the crumbs, add mayo & seasoning, then toss to combine.

Shape into 4 patties.

Heat a pan on medium & fry the patties in a little butter until cooked through, turning halfway (9 min).

Serve on the cut open buns with lettuce & tartar sauce.

Eggplant Parmesan Burgers

Not everyone appreciates a good eggplant (aka aubergine/brinjal, depending on where you were raised). Try this recipe on them & see if you can change their minds.

Serves: 2
Time to Prepare: 15 min

Ingredients

Eggplant:

- ½ Tsp Oil
- 1 Egg White, Stirred & in a Little Dish
- ½ cup Panko Bread Crumbs
- 1 Tbsp & 1 Tbsp of Grated Parmesan Cheese (2 in total)
- ¼ Tsp Pepper
- ¼ Tsp Dried Parsley
- 4 x ½–" Thick Slices of Eggplant (Peeled)

Patties:

- 8 oz Ground Beef
- A Dash of Garlic Powder
- Yet Another Egg White
- ½ cup Marinara Sauce, Warmed Up
- 1 oz Grated Mozzarella Cheese (¼ cup)
- 1 cup Arugula Leaves (aka Rocket)

Directions

Prep:

- Bring your charcoal/gas grill to medium hot.

- Preheat oven to 375°F & grease an oven–proof dish/baking sheet with oil.

Eggplant coating:

- Grab a shallow bowl & mix a ⅓ cup of the panko, 1 Tbsp of the Parmesan, a dash of black pepper, & the parsley flakes.
- Dip each eggplant slice in the egg white first & then into the crumb mixture, then onto the prepared dish/sheet. Lightly spray some cooking spray over the lot.

- Bake until golden & crispy, turning them once (30 min)

Patties:

- While the eggplant is crisping & cooking, mix the meat up with remaining panko, the second tablespoon of Parmesan & the second egg white. Add a dash of pepper & the garlic powder.

- Divide this mix up into 4 patties: ½" thick

- Pop them onto the grill, directly above the heat, cover & grill until internal temp is 160°F, turning once (8–10 min).

To serve:

- Top each golden slice of eggplant with a patty & some marinara sauce. Sprinkle mozzarella over each one & top with arugula.

Pepper Burger with Mushroom–Merlot Gravy

Classy, ahem!

Serves: 6
Time to Prepare: 20 min

Ingredients

Burger:

- 2 lbs Ground Beef
- 2 Tbsp Black Pepper

Mushroom Gravy:

- 3 Tbsp Oil
- 4 cups Assorted Sliced Mushrooms
- 3 Tbsp Finely Sliced Shallots
- 3 Cloves Garlic, Finely Chopped
- 1 Tbsp Flour
- ½ cup Dry Red Wine
- ½ cup Beef Broth
- 1 Tsp Freshly Snipped Thyme
- 2 Tbsp Brandy/Cognac
- 2 Tbsp Unsalted Butter
- Salt & Pepper

To Serve:

- 2–3 cups Arugula (Rocket) or Watercress
- 6 Hamburger Buns, Cut Open & Toasted
- ½ cup Crumbled Up Blue Cheese (Roughly 2 oz)

Directions

Prep:

- Shape the meat into 6 x ¾" thick burger patties. Season one side of the patty with black pepper (coarsely ground is good) & press it into the meat a little. Cover & pop them into the fridge for half an hour.

- **Tip:** you can do this the night before. The patties will keep for 24 hrs.

- Get your charcoal or gas grill preheating to a medium heat while you prepare the gravy.

Gravy:

- Heat an oiled pan over a med–high heat & cook the mushrooms – without stirring – until golden (3–4 min). Now add the shallots & garlic & stir-fry for a few minutes more (2–3 min). Sprinkle flour over the pan & stir to coat everything. Be very careful not to burn...

- Now add the wine & stir up the tasty bits off the bottom of the pan. Bring the wine to the boil, reduce the heat to med–low & simmer until nearly all the liquid is gone, but not all (3–4 min).

- Carefully pour in the stock/broth & the thyme & bring back up to the boil. Reduce the heat once this point has been reached & simmer until thickened (2–3 min). Take the pan off the heat for a moment & carefully add Cognac & butter.

- Return to heat again & stir gently until butter is melted. Season to taste & keep it warm. You will use it in a moment.

Burgers:

- Season the patties with salt. Grill directly over the heat, covered, on an oiled rack. Turn once. Internal temp should be 160–165°F when ready (16–18 min).

To serve:

- Lay the arugula on the bun bottoms. Top that with patties & the mushroom gravy. Sprinkle with blue cheese & perch the tops on top of this tasty concoction.

- Enjoy!

Veggie Burger with Cheese

This is a tasty meat–alternative burger & is fairly low in glycemic load. Fry these up in your kitchen, but you could also do them on the grill outside.

Serves: 4
Time to Prepare: 20 min

Ingredients

Patties:

* 1 Can (14 oz) Black/Red Beans/Chickpeas, Drained (2 cups)
* 1 Medium Onion, Cut into Rough Wedges
* ½ cup Oats (Rolled)
* 1 Tbsp Chili Powder
* A Dash of Salt
* Freshly Ground Black Pepper
* ½–1 cup Grated Cheese: Parmesan/Cheddar/Swiss/Mozzarella

Extras:

* Liquid from Cooking the Beans/Stock/Water As Needed
* 1 Tbsp Oil, for Cooking

Toppings:

* The Usual Suspects (Lettuce, tomato, onion)

Directions

Get the patty ingredients together (beans, onions, oats, chili powder, salt, pepper, & cheese) in a food processor & pulse lightly until chunky (mash, not mush).

If it seems a little on the dry side, add some of the liquid from the bean can little bit by little. You want moist, not wet concoction going there.

Let the mix sit in the fridge or for a bit until it is firm enough to handle. Then make your four patties & put it back in the fridge for as long as you can (20 min if possible).

Tip: Use wet hands for the shaping process.

To cook:

- Heat your pan on med–high & coat with oil. Fry the patties until brown (10 min) – turning only once.

Serve:

- Serve on hamburger rolls with your favorite toppings.

Philly Cheesesteak Burger

The burger version of this famous steak. The topping includes fried mushroom, sweet peppers, & onions.

Serves: 6
Time to Prepare: 15 min

Ingredients

Burger Patties:

- 1½ lb Ground Beef (Sirloin, if you want to be more authentic)

Toppings:

- 1 Tbsp Oil – Olive or Canola
- 1 Large Onion
- 1 Sweet Red Pepper, Insides Removed & Sliced Up
- ½ lb Button Mushrooms, Sliced

To Serve:

- 12 Thin Slices of Cheese, Preferably Provolone (±6 oz)
- Pepperoncini (For fun & as garnish)
- ¾ lb Italian Bread Cut into Six Segments, Each Segment Cut Open Like a Hamburger Bun… or Just Use Hamburger Buns

Directions

Prep:

- Get the coals going. You want med–hot coals or a med–hot gas grill (preheat on high & then drop the temp to med–hot). Grease the rack you plan to use.

Patties:

- Form the meat into six patties & pop in the fridge for later.

Now prepare the topping:

- Fry the onions alone in 1 Tbsp of oil for around 5 min over a med–hot stove. Then add the peppers & mushrooms & cook until tender (4–5 min).

Grilling:

- Cover (if using a gas grill) & grill until the internal temp is 160°F (6 min). Turn off heat & quickly place 2 slices of cheese on the top of each one. Wait until the cheese melts before serving.

Serving:

- Put each burger on a piece of Italian bread & spoon the topping over it. Serve with pepperoncini for an extra point on the Universal Scale of Tastiness.

Relish the All–American Burger

It's a well, burger. But not just any ole' burger… This one will be your go–to recipe when you need something a bit more interesting than a plain patty on a bun.

Serves: 4
Time to Prepare: 25 min

Ingredients

Relish:

*   ½ cup Roasted Red Pepper, Sliced
*   1 Tbsp Finely Chopped Olives
*   2 Tsp Oil
*   2 Tsp Freshly Snipped Thyme (or ½ Tsp dried)
*   ¼ Tsp Black Pepper

Burger:

*   ¼ cup Finely Chopped Onion
*   2 Tbsp Bread Crumbs
*   2 Tbsp Ketchup
*   1 Tbsp Horseradish Paste
*   1 Tbsp Mustard
*   ¼ Tsp Salt
*   ¼ Tsp Pepper
*   1 lb Ground Beef
*   4 Slices Smoked Mozzarella Cheese (or Not smoked; preference)

To Serve:

*   4 Hamburger Buns, Cut Open & Toasted Lightly
*   Fresh Basil Leaves

Directions

Prep:

*   Get your grill (gas or charcoal) to a good medium heat. The coals will be ready when they have a layer of gray ash on them.

For the relish:

- Pop the pepper strips, olives, oil, thyme, & ¼ Tsp of black pepper into a food processor, mix a little before pulsing. You want the food chopped, not liquidized, so be careful. Cover this & leave it to chill in the fried until serving time.

The burgers:

- Mix up the onions bread crumbs, ketchup, horseradish, mustard, salt, & the second ¼ Tsp pepper in a bowl. Add the meat & mix until just combined. Divide this mix into 4 patties that are roughly ¾" thick

To cook:

- Pop the patties onto an oiled grill rack & cook until the internal temp is 160°F (16–18 min). Remember to turn only once halfway through cooking. Just before you take the meat off, lay a slice of cheese on the top of each one so that it can melt a bit.

Serve:

- Serve on a toasted bun with fresh basil & 1 Tbsp of per bun of red sweet pepper relish.

Classic Veal Burgers

If you like the taste of game meat, this one is for you: good spices, rye bread & swiss cheese

Serves: 4
Time to Prepare: 20 min

Ingredients

Burger:

- 1 Egg, Lightly Beaten with a Fork
- 2 Tbsp Water (or Beer, if you happen to have some)
- 1 Slice Rye Bread Turned into Crumbs (¾ cup)
- ½ Tsp Caraway Seeds
- ½ Tsp Dried Marjoram
- 1 Clove Garlic, Finely Sliced
- ¼ Tsp Salt
- ¼ Tsp Black Pepper
- 1 lb Ground Beef

To Serve:

- 8 Slices of Rye Bread (9 slices in total, one was for making crumbs)
- 4 x 1 oz Slices Swiss Cheese
- 3 Tbsp Mustard of Choice

Directions

Prep:

- Get your grill (gas of charcoal) to a good medium heat.

Patties:

- Stir together the egg & water/beer, then add the crumbs, caraway, marjoram, garlic, & seasoning. Now mix the meat in well & shape into four patties: ¾" thick.

Cook:

- Pop the patties on an oiled grill rack, directly over the heat. Grill (uncovered) until the internal temp is 160°F (16–18 min) turning once halfway.

- Just before you remove the burgers, add the bread to the grill & toast one side lightly (1–2 min). Turn them, put a slice of cheese on four of them & toast the bottoms (1–2 min).

To serve:

- Serve the cheese–topped bread with the patties on top. Then spread the un–cheesed ones with mustard & close the burger.

Berry Peachy Turkey

This is the epitome of creative. Give this show-stopper a try!

Serves: 4
Time to Prepare: 30 min

Ingredients

Burger:

- 1 lb Ground Turkey
- Salt & Pepper
- 4 Slices of Cheese (Monterey jack)
- 4 Peaches

Peach Mix:

- ½ cup of Fresh Blueberries
- ¼ Tsp Chili Powder
- 4 Man-sized Slices of Garlic Bread (Try them toasted)
- Freshly Plucked Mint Leaves

Directions

Take one peach & chop it into tiny, little bits.

Then mix it together with the turkey & seasoning. You are now ready to shape into patties: 4 x ½" thick.

Tip: Wet your hands a bit before handling.

Set your grill to med-high & pop the patties onto a rack directly over the heat. Cook until there is no more pink inside; internal temp 165°F (roughly 5 min/side).

While you wait for the meat to cook, locate the other three peaches & chop them coarsely (but neatly). Get the blueberries, chili powder & peaches cooking on medium until they are nicely warmed; this will be just as the juices start to appear (5 min).

When the patties are ready, put the cheese on top, cover & cook on the grill again until it has melted just a bit (1 min).

Assembling:

- 1st Layer: Garlic bread

- 2nd Layer: Turkey burger with melted cheese

- 3rd Layer: Chili–peach mix

- 4th Layer: A little mint leaf or two

- Final Layer: If you like, sprinkle a light dusting of chili powder over the lot to garnish.

Montreal Tuna Burger

Here is another take on the steak au poivre, merely a fancy term for "pepper steak"

Serves: 6
Time to Prepare: 15 min

Ingredients

- ½ cup Sour Cream
- 2 Tbsp Chopped Parsley
- 2 Tsp Chopped Shallots
- 1 Tsp Honey Dijon Mustard
- 6 x 4 oz Tuna Steaks (1" Thick)
- 6 Large Slices Sourdough Bread Cut in Half Crosswise
- 2 Tsp Montreal Steak Seasoning
- 1 Small Bunch of Chicory/Endive Leaves

Directions

Prep:

- Get whichever grilling method you prefer to a good medium–heat. Oil or spray the rack you will be using.

Sour cream sauce:

- Combine the sour cream, parsley, chopped shallots & honey mustard. Cover & keep in the fridge until serving time – which is only one paragraph away.

Cook it:

- Rub both sides of tuna with Montreal seasoning. Grill for 6 minutes in total, turning once. Keep the cooked tuna warm on a plate.

Assemble it:

- Spread the cream mix onto the top portions of the buns, then lay the tuna & endives inside before closing & serving.

- Spread top of each bread slice with 2 Tsp of sour cream mixture. Sandwich a tuna steak & some frisee between bread slices & serve.

Potato Mini's

Use baked waffle–cut potatoes in place on buns. This would be an excellent dish to serve to a small crowd as a little appetizer. Enlist some help & make a double batch.

Serves: 16
Time to Prepare: 15 min

Ingredients

- 16 Large Frozen Waffle–cut Potatoes (⅓ of a 22 oz package)
- 1 lb Ground Beef (Can also use turkey)
- 3 Tsp Your Favorite Grill Seasoning
- 4 Slices of Cheddar Cheese, Each Cut into 4 Pieces (4 oz)
- 4 Sliced Cherry Tomatoes
- Various Condiments (Ketchup, mustard, sour cream, pickles)

Directions

Prep:

- Preheat oven to 400°F.

Potatoes:

- Line a baking sheet with foil & space the potatoes out on it. Bake until lightly browned & crispy (18 min).

Burgers:

- While this is going, mix the meat & seasoning. Make 16 little mini burgers & fry them up on a med–high heat until internal temperature is 160°F (5 min). Turn once. Drain on kitchen paper towels.

- Once the potatoes are done, set them aside & move the oven racks to roughly 5" from the element (don't forget to adjust the oven to broil to preheat).

Now assemble:

- Now grab one potato waffle thingy & top with a burger, a dinky little piece of cheese & a slice of tomato. Repeat x 16.

- Broil briefly for a minute or two until it looks tasty.

Serve:

- Serve with your usual condiments like mustard & ketchup along with sour cream & pickles. Watch them disappear! :)

Caribbean Chicken Burger

An interesting mix of flavors guaranteed to inspire you

Serves: 4
Time to Prepare: 20 min

Ingredients

Burgers:

- 2 Slices of Bread – Ripped into Chunks for Making Crumbs
- 1 lb Ground Chicken
- ½ cup Whole Milk
- 1 Tsp Onion Powder or Onion Soup Powder
- 1 Tsp Salt
- ¼ Tsp Thyme
- 8 Slices Sourdough Bread
- ½ Tsp Allspice (Nutmeg, cinnamon & clove in equal quantities)

Mango Relish:

- 2 Tbsp Finely Chopped Onion
- 1 Tbsp Wine Vinegar (Red)
- 1 Tsp Sugar
- Pinch of Salt
- 1 Medium–sized Mango, Flesh Diced (1 cup)
- 1 Tbsp Freshly Chopped Cilantro

Directions

Burgers:

- Get the grill/or coals to a good medium heat.

- Make fresh breadcrumbs by pulsing the bread bits in a food processor & keep aside for a minute. Now to pulse the patty ingredients (ground chicken, whole milk, onion powder, salt, & spices) until just combined, then add the crumbs you just made. Shape into 4 neat patties.

Mango Relish:

- To make the relish, you will need a microwavable bowl to mix together the onion, vinegar, sugar, & salt. Nuke on high for a minute & leave it to cool for at least 30 sec.

- Once, cooled a little, stir in the mango bits & chopped cilantro.

To cook:

- Brush the patties with oil or coat with cooking spray. Grill for 8 min, turning only once. It should be cooked through.

- Just before the cooking time is up, grill the bread. Serve everything together with the tasty relish.

Creole-styled Meat-Free Burger

Grab a known carnivore & have them see what they think of this one

Serves: 4
Time to Prepare: 15 min

Ingredients

The Patties:

- 1 x Can (15 oz) Red Kidney Beans: Rinsed & Mashed
- 1 Onion, Sliced
- 1 Egg (Raw, for binding)
- 1 Tbsp Tomato Sauce/Ketchup
- 1 Tsp Mustard (Pre–made)
- 2 Tsp Worcestershire Sauce
- ¼ Tsp Cumin (Ground)
- 3 Tbsp Bread Crumbs (Flavored ones can be used)

To Serve:

- 1 Tbsp Vegetable Oil (For frying)
- 4 x Buns
- Lettuce
- Thousand Island Salad Dressing

Directions

Mix all the ingredients & form into 4 patties.

Heat oil in a pan over a med–low heat. Fry for 3 min/side.

Serve with buns & lettuce with dressing.

Asian Chicken Burger

The chicken is not from Asia. But the concept is!

Serves: 4
Time to Prepare: 15 mins

Ingredients

- 6 Finely Sliced Scallions (Include some of the green)
- 1 x Drained 8 oz Can of Water Chestnuts, Chopped
- ½ cup Sweet & Sour Duck Sauce (Orange sauce)
- 2 Tbsp Oil of Choice
- 2 oz Shiitake Mushrooms, Chopped
- 1 Clove Garlic, Finely Chopped
- 1 lb Ground Chicken
- 2 Tbsp Freshly Chopped Cilantro
- 1 Tbsp Soy Sauce
- ¼ Tsp Salt
- A Dash of Black Pepper
- 4 Sesame Seed Round Buns, Best Served Warm

Directions

Mix roughly 2 Tbsp of the sliced scallions with an equal amount of chopped chestnuts & duck sauce.

Fry up the mushrooms, remaining scallions & garlic until they look tender (3 min). Leave it to cool a little & then add the mushroom mix with the chicken, remaining chestnut, cilantro & soy sauce in a bowl

Make up four patties about ¾" thick. Season the tops of the patties with a little salt & pepper.

Fry the patties in the recently abandoned pan (salted side down); med–heat. Sprinkle some more salt & pepper on them. Cook until 165°F (16–18 min), gently turning once.

Pop a burger in each warmed bun, garnish with a cilantro sprig & a side of sauce. And there you have it!

Blue Stuffed Burgers with Onion & Spinach

If you like blue cheese, this one if for you. If not, feel free to substitute the blue for your favorite variety.

Serves: 4
Time to Prepare: 25 min

Ingredients

Burgers:

- 1 lb Ground Beef
- 1 Tbsp Worcestershire Sauce
- 1 Tsp Black Pepper
- ½ cup Crumbled Blue Cheese (2 oz)

Trimmings:

- 1 Med–size Onion, Sliced Thinly (Red are generally sweeter)
- A Splash or Two of Olive Oil for Brushing
- Salt to Taste

To Serve:

- 4 Hamburger Buns, Cut Open
- 1 cup Baby Spinach Leaves (Fresh, not frozen)

Directions

Prep:

- Get your grill ready to go at a medium heat – no need to preheat because you will be cooking the meat uncovered. This would apply to a charcoal grill as well.

The patty:

- Mix the meat, Worcestershire sauce, & pepper in a large bowl.

- Divide the mix into 8 balls. Pat them out until they are nice & thin: 4″ in diameter. Half of these are tops, the other half tails.

- Put 1 Tbsp of cheese on 4 of the patties. Toss a coin to see which side will get it, then match it with its mate & pinch the edges to seal it.

- Brush onion rings with oil & scatter salt on them.

Now cook:

- Grill burgers & onions on an oiled rack, directly over med–high heat. Grill until done: internal temp of 160°–165°F (5 min).

- Brush the cut faces of the buns with oil & toast them in the last few moments of grilling the meat.

To serve:

- Serve on hamburger buns with the onion, spinach, & any remaining cheese.

Home On the Range

Here is a recipe with a bit of zing to it. It has apples, bison, cantaloupes, strawberries, cayenne pepper & citrus zest among other amazing ingredient combos. If one eyebrow is up in the air in shock, read on… all will be revealed.

Serves: 6
Time to Prepare: 30 min

Ingredients

Apple Mix:

- 1 Small Granny Smith Apple, Finely Chopped (½ cup)
- 1 Small Stalk of Celery, Finely Sliced (⅓ cup)
- 1 Tiny Onion, Finely Sliced (⅓ cup)
- 1 Tbsp Olive Oil

Burgers:

- 3 Tbsp Ketchup
- 1 Tsp Jerk Seasoning
- ¼ Tsp Salt
- ¼ Tsp Ground Black Pepper or Cayenne Pepper
- 1½ lb Uncooked Ground Bison or Lean Ground Beef

To Serve:

- 6 Man–sized Slices of Rustic Bread
- ¼ cup Melted Butter
- Red–tipped Leaf Lettuce

Melon Relish:

- 1 Small Orange–fleshed Melon: Flesh Chopped (1 cup)
- 4 oz Chopped Strawberries (1 cup)
- 1 Tiny Red Onion, Finely Chopped Up (¼ cup)
- 1 Tiny Sweet Green Pepper, Finely Chopped Up (¼ cup)
- 2 Tbsp Freshly Chopped Cilantro
- 1 Tbsp Freshly Snipped Mint Leaves
- 1 Tsp Lemon or Lime Zest (Squeeze juice out after zesting)
- 2 Tbsp Lemon or Lime Juice

Directions

Apple mix:

- Fry apple, celery & onion in hot oil over med–heat until mixture is tender (6–8 min); then leave it to cool down to room temperature.

Burger:

- Grab a large bowl & pop the apple mixture, ketchup, & all the seasoning. Add the meat (bison/beef) & mix well. Divide into six ¾" thick burger patties.

And cook:

- Charcoal: Grill patties on a well–oiled rack of an open grill directly over med–hot coals until no longer pink; internal temp 160°F (16–18 min). Turning once, halfway.

- Gas grill: Preheat & drop the heat to med–hot. Grill as above.

- Just before removing the meat, toast the bread on both sides. Brush with melted butter when you're done.

And serve:

- Top the toast with lettuce, patties & melon relish.

Melon relish:

- Combine the chopped melon, strawberries, onion, sweet pepper, cilantro, fresh mint, lemon/lime zest & juice. Toss lightly to coat everything in the juice.

- Leave it to sit at room temperature for half an hour or so, stirring now & then. This way the flavors will combine.

- **Tip:** You can prepare this the night before & leave it in the fridge for 4–24 hrs. Then let it stand at room temp for 30 min.

Juicy Lucy Burger

A Juicy Lucy burger (traditionally) is a burger stuffed with cheese. Make sure that it has cooled somewhat before attempting to bite it. The cheese & steam may burn you.

Serves: 6
Time to Prepare: 35 min

Ingredients

Burger Patty:

- 1 cup of Breadcrumbs
- ½ cup of Whole Milk (or Beef broth for a tasty, dairy–free option)
- 1 Egg
- ¼ cup Seasoned Bread Crumbs
- 2 Tbsp Worcestershire Sauce
- ¾ Tsp Salt
- ½ Tsp Freshly Ground Black Pepper
- 2 lbs Ground Beef
- 12 x ¾ oz Slices of Cheese (American or swiss) Cut into 4 Pieces

To Serve:

- 6 Large Hamburger Buns
- Condiments of Your Choosing (Pickles, ketchup, relish)

Directions

Soak the soft bread crumbs in milk for a few minutes before adding in the egg & dry crumbs along with Worcestershire sauce & seasoning. Now add the meat & mix very gently.

Divide the mix into 12 balls & pat half of them down to roughly ½" thick & 3½" wide. These are the "lids". The remaining six will form the "pots" that you will pop your cheese into: just push a depression into the ball with the bottom of a drinking glass. Fill & seal the whole lot up & pinch the edges together.

Variation: Add any kind of yummy stuff to the cheese, like sliced jalapeños. Just make sure you have enough space in the "pots".

Pop into the fridge for an hour (at least), so they can firm up before cooking them.

For the charcoal grill:

- Cook over med–hot coals (place a drip pan below them in case of spillage). Grill for roughly 14 minutes. Turn carefully & continue grilling for 12 minutes (160°F)

For gas:

- Preheat & drop the heat to med–hot. Cook as for charcoal grill, only cover the patties.

- Toast the buns (open face down) for the last minute or so of cooking.

To serve:

- DO NOT EAT RIGHT AWAY! This could result in much unhappiness – especially for children. Let the burgers stand for a few minutes to let the cheese cool a bit first.

- Serve in the buns with your favorite condiments & toppings (pickles, relish, etc).

Blue Vidalia Burgers

Vidalia may bring computer software to the minds of some, but to others, it is a particularly sweet kind of onion. For the purposes of this recipe, we'll stick with the edible onion version.

Serves: 8
Time to Prepare: 30 min

Ingredients

Onion Parcel:

- 2 Large, Sweet (Vidalia) Onions, Cut into Thick Slices
- 1 Tbsp Butter

Patties:

- 2 lbs Ground Beef
- ¾ Tsp Salt
- ¼ Tsp Black Pepper

The Rest:

- 1 cup (4 oz) Crumbled Blue Cheese
- 4 oz Cream Cheese
- 2 Tsp Worcestershire Sauce
- ½ Tsp Black Pepper
- ½ Tsp Dried Dill Weed – Leaves & Stems (Also known as dill)
- 8 Hamburger Buns, Cut Open (Toasted if You Like)

Directions

Prep:

- Bring your charcoal to medium heat or preheat your gas grill on full before dropping the setting to med–high. The gas grill will be covered during cooking.

The onions:

- Obtain a 36"x18" piece of heavy–duty foil & fold it in half to make a really strong, foil square. Pack the onions & dots of butter in the center, bring the foil edges over & make a sealed parcel. Don't wrap them too tightly though.

- Grill the package directly over the heat until the onions are just tender. Turn the foil package now & then (25–30 min).

Patties:

- While you wait for the onions to cook, mix up the meat & seasoning. Divide into 8 balls & pat them down until ¾" thick.

- Grill them on a lightly oiled rack until the internal temp is 160°F, turning once (14–18min)

Serve & trim:

- Mix together: blue cheese, cream cheese, Worcestershire sauce, pepper, & dill. Lift the onions out of their foil bed (leave any juice behind) & toss to coat.

- Spoon this mixture over the burgers in buns.

Chicken BBQ Burger

Use minced chicken & corn instead of beef. This recipe uses & extra bun for making bread crumbs; so if you have some ready–made stuff on hand you would rather use, you only need 6 buns.

Serves: 6
Time to Prepare: 5 min

Ingredients

The Burger:

- 1 Small Chopped Onion (1 cup)
- 1 Tsp Your Vegetable Oil of Choice
- 6 (+1 Extra) Round Buns (+1 Extra bun for the food processor)
- 1 lb Ground Chicken
- 1 Egg, Lightly Beaten
- 3 Tbsp Your Favorite Barbecue Sauce
- ½ Tsp Salt
- ¼ Tsp Ground Black Pepper
- 1 cup Corn Kernels (Fresh or thawed from frozen)

To Serve:

- Sliced Red Onion
- Barbecue Sauce

Directions

Charcoal:

- Med–hot coals

Gas grill:

- Med–hot

Broil:

- Heat oven broiler & give the rack a poof or two of cooking spray

Sauté onion on med–low until softened (10 min) but don't let them brown.

While the onions are sweating away, savagely rip a bun apart & pop into a food processor. Pulse until there is nothing left but fine crumbs.

Mix the ground chicken, lightly beaten egg, & the rest of the burger ingredients together. Shape into 6 balls & then pat them into, well, patties.

Grill or broil roughly 4″ from the heat. Turn after about 5 min. & cook until done (165°F), which will take another 5 min or so.

Serve with the rolls, garnishing with onion slices & extra sauce & any of your favorite trimmings.

Thai Turkey Burgers

Turkey burger dress code: bun, salsa, peanuts & Thai

Serves: 4
Time to Prepare: 45 min

Ingredients

Peanut Sauce:

* 2 Tbsp Peanut Butter
* 1 Tbsp Rice Vinegar
* 1 Tbsp Soy Sauce
* 1½ Tsp Freshly Grated Ginger
* 1 Tsp Sesame Oil (Dark or light)
* ½ Tsp Pure Honey

Mango Salsa:

* 1 Ripe Mango: the Flesh Cubed
* ¼ cup Chopped Sweet Red Pepper
* 2 Tbsp Lime Juice (Freshly squeezed, if possible)
* 2 Tbsp Freshly Chopped Cilantro
* 1 Tbsp Freshly Chopped Basil
* 2 Tsp Oil
* Salt & Pepper to Taste

Burgers:

* 1 lb Ground Turkey
* 2 Tbsp Sliced Green Onions
* 2 Tbsp Freshly Chopped Cilantro
* 2 Tbsp Peanut Sauce (The one you made just now)

Serve:
* 4 Hamburger Buns, Cut Open & Toasted Lightly

Directions

Prep:

* Heat grill to medium–high.

Peanut Sauce:

- Mix the ingredients (peanut butter, vinegar, soy sauce, sesame oil, honey, fresh ginger) in a bowl & set aside.

Mango Salsa:

- Mix the ingredients for the mango salsa (mango cubes, red pepper, lime, cilantro, basil, oil & seasoning) together in a bowl & set aside.

Burgers:

- Mix the turkey, green onions, cilantro, & 2 Tbsp of the peanut sauce. Divide the mixture in four & shape into patties: ½″ thick. Spray both sides of the burgers with cooking spray.

Cook:

- Grill until cooked through & the internal temp is 165°F (10 min). Turn halfway.

Serve:

- Pop the burgers on the buns with the freshly made mango salsa & peanut sauce.

Salad Blues

A burger with a salad complex. Or a salad masquerading as a burger... who knows!

Serves: 4
Time to Prepare: 15 min

Ingredients

Dressing:

- 3 Tbsp Unfiltered Apple Cider Vinegar
- 3 Tbsp Oil
- ½ Tsp Dried Rosemary
- ¼ Tsp Dried Thyme
- ¼ Tsp Salt
- ¼ Tsp Pepper

Things to Cook:

- 2 Slices Red Onion (¼" Thick)
- 4 Patties (Meat or vegetarian)

To Serve:

- 6 cups Roughly Ripped Romaine Lettuce
- 1 oz Blue Cheese Crumbled Up
- 2 Tbsp Toasted, Chopped Walnuts

Directions

Dressing:

- Throw the dressing ingredients (vinegar, oil, herbs & spices) into a jar or bottle with a good lid. Do the "happy & you know it" dance if you are happy & you know it, keeping a firm grip on the bottle. Otherwise, if people are watching, just mix it up in a cup.

Burgers & onion:

- Brush onion on both sides with a bit of dressing. Grill the onion & frozen burgers over med–hot until cooked (4–6 minutes). Turn once only.

To serve:

- Distribute the lettuce between the plates.

- Cut the burgers up into strips & pop on top of the lettuce with the onion rings. Add the blue cheese & walnuts to complete the picture & drizzle with dressing.

- And there you go. Both girls & boys will be able to appreciate this meal.

Caramelized Onion Turkey Burger

This is the ultimate turkey burger, sporting caramelized onions & blue cheese. Can't get much better than this!

Serves: 4
Time to Prepare: 15 min

Ingredients

Onions:

- 1 Tbsp Butter
- 1 Large Sweet Onion, Sliced Thinly

Burger:

- 1 Bag of Ground Turkey (20 oz)
- ½ cup Ricotta Cheese
- 1¾ Tsp Worcestershire Sauce
- 1¾ Tsp Dijon–style Mustard
- ¼ Tsp Salt
- ¼ Tsp Freshly Ground Black Pepper
- 1 Tbsp Oil (Whichever variety you prefer)

- Blue Mix:

- 1 oz Crumbled Up Blue Cheese (¼ cup)
- 2 Tbsp Mayo
- 4 Hamburger Buns
- 4 Lettuce Leaves

Directions

Onions:

- Heat a pan to medium–high & melt the butter. Cook until well browned, but not burned (15 min). Keep one side for later.

Burgers:

- Stir together the turkey, ricotta cheese, Worcestershire sauce, mustard, & seasoning. Divide into 4 & shape into flat patties.

Cook:

- Cook over a medium heat in a large pan, 5 min/side. Cover partially & set the heat at medium. Cook for another 5 min (160°F)

To serve:

- While burgers do their thing, stir the blue cheese & mayo together in a small bowl.

- Pop the burgers into the rolls & top with some onions, blue cheese sauce & lettuce.

25744507R00055

Printed in Great Britain
by Amazon